SIGN
Language
for Kids

A Fun & Easy Guide to American Sign Language

Lora Heller

Sterling Publishing Co., Inc.
New York

Acknowledgments

This book was a pleasure to write and develop. There are a few people I would like to thank, without whom this book would not have happened: Heather Quinlan of Sterling, for finding me, trusting in me, and supporting my work. Hazel Chan of Sterling, my wonderful editor, for being so patient, persistent, and professional. Michael Hnatov, our creative and insightful photographer—the kids and I all had a blast working with you. Gina DiBartolomeo, for her support, friendship, and ASL guidance.

A special thank you to our wonderful models: Matthew (in royal blue), Anna (in dark green), Molly (in red), Ian (in red), David (in light blue), and Rebekah (in lime green). The six of you bring life to this book! I could not have asked for more beautiful and expressive faces to help teach other kids these signs.

A thank you in advance to the kids who do learn from this book. I hope your process is as fun as mine was.

Last, but definitely not least, thank you to my husband, Ian, and my children, Zeke and Sian. You guys helped me stay focused in my work and you always remind me of the important things in life. I love you.

—Lora Heller

Library of Congress Cataloging-in-Publication Data

Heller, Lora
    Sign Language for kids : a fun & easy guide to American sign language
/ Lora Heller
        p. cm
     Includes index.
     Summary: Color photos illustrate sign language for numbers, letters, colors,
feelings, animals, and clothes.
     ISBN 1-4027-0672-3
     1. Sign language—Juvenile literature. [1. Sign language.] I. Title.
HV2476 .H45   2004
419' .7—dc22

2003019011

10 9 8 7 6 5 4 3 2

Published by Sterling Publishing Co., Inc.
387 Park Avenue South, New York, NY 10016
© 2004 by Lora Heller
Distributed in Canada by Sterling Publishing
c/o Canadian Manda Group, 165 Dufferin Street,
Toronto, Ontario, Canada M6K 3H6
Distributed in Great Britain and Europe by Chris Lloyd at Orca Book
Services, Stanley House, Fleets Lane, Poole BH15 3AJ, England
Distributed in Australia by Capricorn Link (Australia) Pty. Ltd.
P.O. Box 704, Windsor, NSW 2756, Australia

Printed in China

Sterling ISBN 1-4027-0672-3

Contents

Learning to Sign

SIGNING IS A fun way to communicate with each other. It is not only used by people who are deaf or hard of hearing. Different people use sign language in many special ways: maybe you and a friend want to have a "secret" way of talking to each other, or there is a new boy in your neighborhood who is deaf and you would like to be his friend, or your friend's sister is deaf and you would like to know a few signs to greet her

when you visit. Sign language has even been used to communicate with animals, such as apes and sea lions. Koko, a very famous ape, learned over 500 signs. (To learn more about Koko, see Resources on the opposite page.)

Whatever the reason, this book will help you learn some American Sign Language (ASL) that you can use at home, school, and with your friends. For each word, you will see the sign, a description of how to make the sign, and a photograph of someone signing the word. You can read the book from start to finish or look for a specific word from the index at the back of the book. It may help to learn all the signs for the alphabet and numbers first, because many of the other words in the book start off with a letter or number sign. You can learn the words either on your own by signing in front of a mirror or with a friend or family member.

Signing is such an expressive way of communicating. Have fun with it!

A Little History

IN 1815, A young pastor named Thomas Hopkins Gallaudet met a 9-year-old deaf girl named Alice Cogswell. Alice's father asked Gallaudet to become her teacher but he first needed to learn how to teach a deaf child. So Gallaudet left Connecticut to study abroad. He first went to England and then to Paris looking for someone to teach him. In Paris, he studied with Sicard, the director of a school for the deaf. When he was finished, Gallaudet came back home with one of Sicard's teachers, Laurent Clerc. In 1817, they opened the American School for the Deaf in Hartford, Connecticut. The school is still there today. Even though deaf Americans were already using some signs, Clerc taught his students combinations of French signs to really develop the language called American Sign Language (ASL). In 1864, Gallaudet University (named after Thomas Gallaudet), in Washington, D.C., became the first college for deaf students. Gallaudet University is still there, and students and teachers continue to use ASL at the university.

Resources for Kids and Parents

- www.gallaudet.edu   **Gallaudet University**
- www.ntd.org   **National Theatre of the Deaf/Little Theatre of the Deaf**
- www.lexnyc.org   **Lexington School for the Deaf**
- www.nysd.org   **New York Society for the Deaf**
- www.koko.org   **Learn more about Koko and ASL**

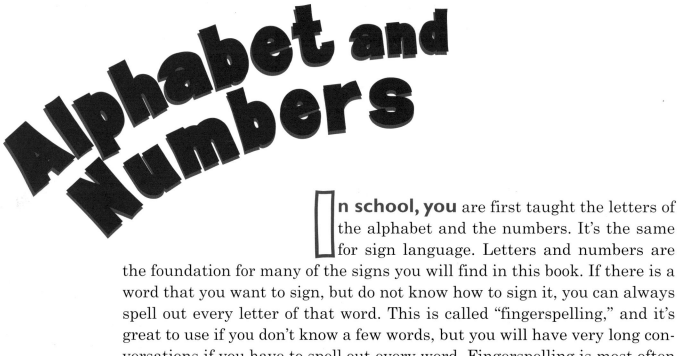

Alphabet and Numbers

In school, you are first taught the letters of the alphabet and the numbers. It's the same for sign language. Letters and numbers are the foundation for many of the signs you will find in this book. If there is a word that you want to sign, but do not know how to sign it, you can always spell out every letter of that word. This is called "fingerspelling," and it's great to use if you don't know a few words, but you will have very long conversations if you have to spell out every word. Fingerspelling is most often used when you want to sign your name or someone else's, or for words that don't have actual signs. If you take it slowly and practice, you'll be soon be going from A to Z. If you are left-handed, just do each sign with your left hand.

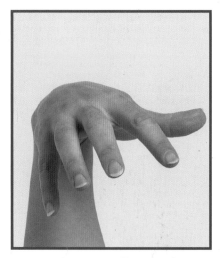

Fingerspelling

With an open palm facing downward, wiggle your fingers side to side in front of your body.

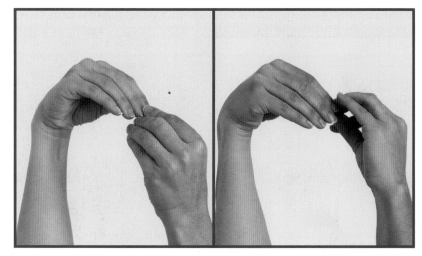

Numbers

With the fingertips of each hand together, bring your hands to meet each other and twist back and forth.

Alphabet

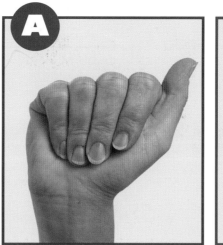

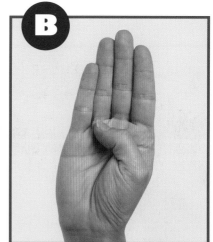

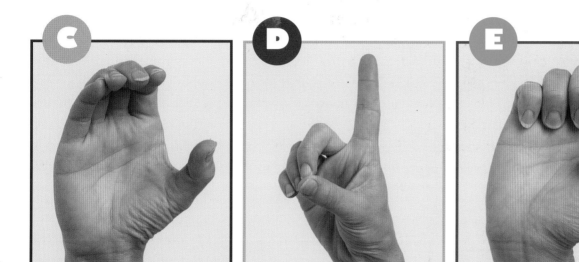

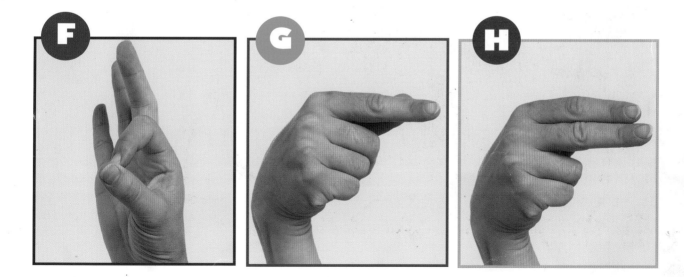

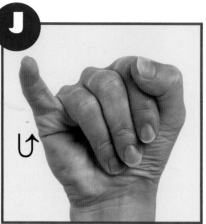

The letter "J" looks correct from your point of view—but to the person you're signing to, it is backwards.

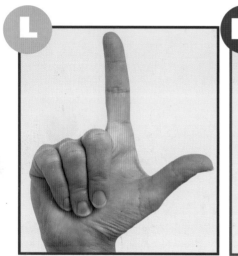

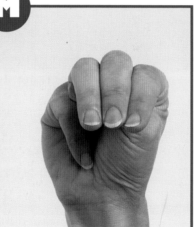

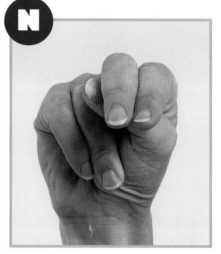

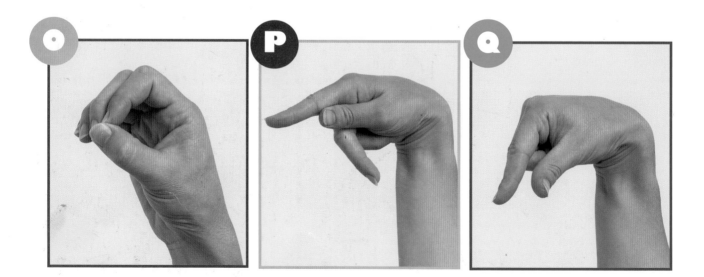

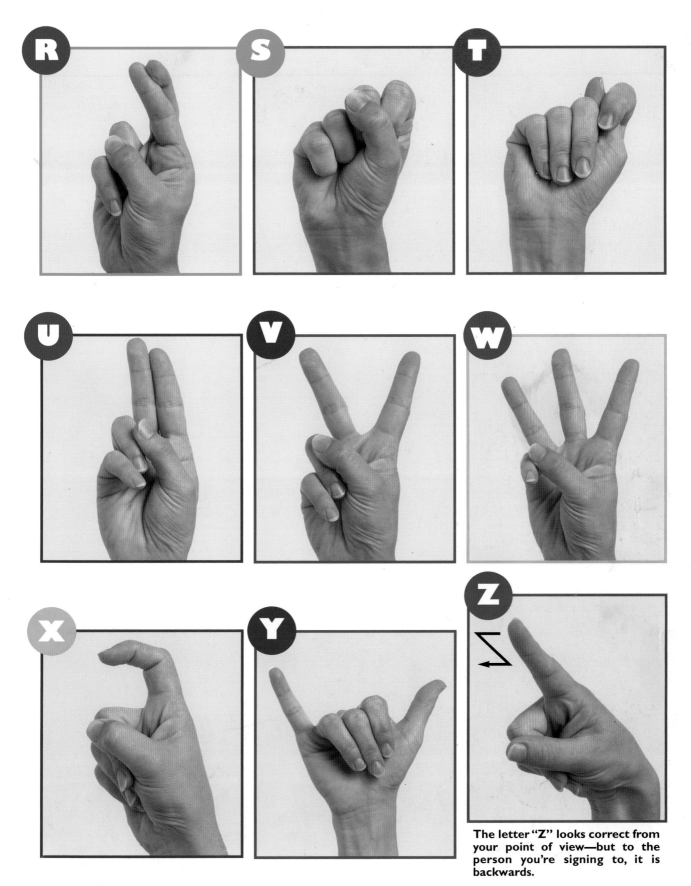

The letter "Z" looks correct from your point of view—but to the person you're signing to, it is backwards.

Alphabet and Numbers 9

Numbers

Counting in **ASL** is different from how you have learned it in school. All your counting is done with one hand. It may seem hard at first, but you will see that there is pattern to forming numbers that will have you counting in no time.

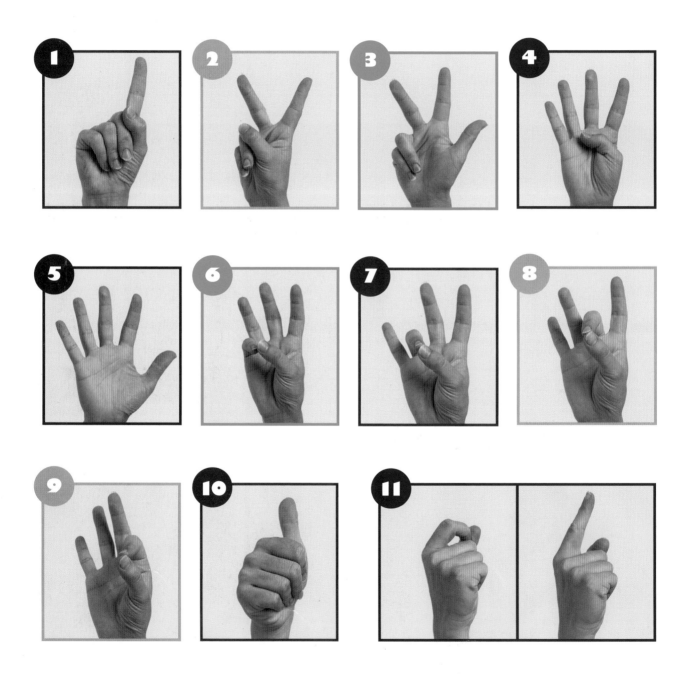

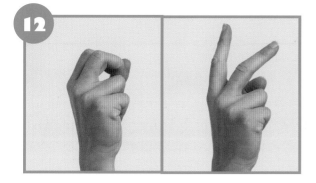

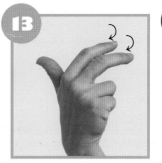

Bend index and middle finger toward palm.

With your thumb tucked in, bend your four other fingers toward your palm.

With your thumb out, bend your four other fingers toward your palm.

Form a "6" hand sign and twist your wrist from side to side.

Form a "7" hand sign and twist your wrist from side to side.

Form an "8" hand sign and twist your wrist from side to side.

Form a "9" hand sign and twist your wrist from side to side.

Open and close your index finger and thumb together.

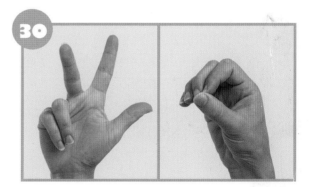

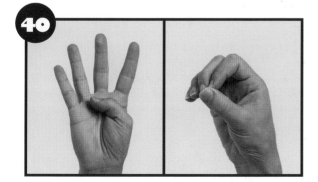

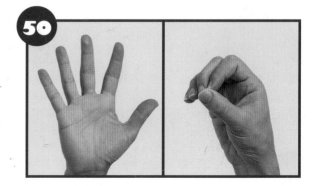

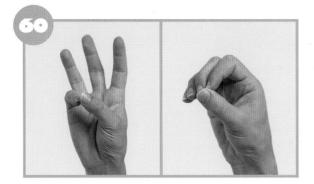

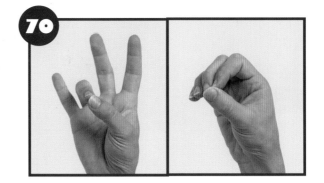

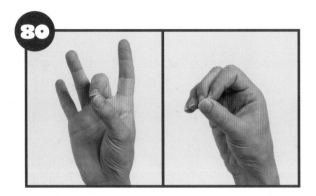

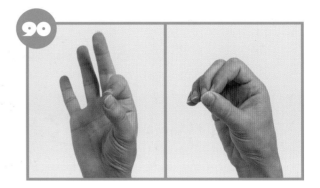

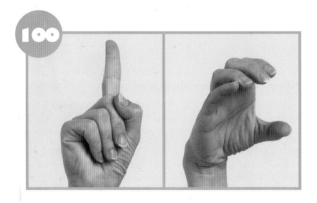

Home, Family, and Pets

The **signs in** this chapter will help you have private conversations with your brother, sister, or friends. You can even train your pet dog to respond to commands in sign language! Many deaf people do this so that their pet can help them around the house. In addition to understanding sign language, the dog acts as the owner's "ears" by waking her up in the morning when the alarm rings, bringing the telephone when there's a call, or taking her to the door when the doorbell rings.

Home
With your fingertips together, first touch the side of your mouth and then your temple.

Family

Begin with two "F" hand signs together, palms facing out. Move your hands away from each other, forming a circle in the air in front of you. End with your palms facing in.

Bathroom/Toilet

Form the letter "T" and shake it.

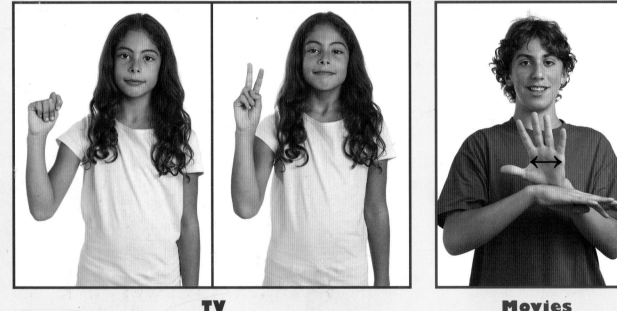

TV

Fingerspell the letter "T" (your thumb comes up between your index and middle fingers) and then the letter "V" (looks like the number 2, or "peace" sign).

Movies

Have one hand open with palm facing down. Rub the palm of the other hand, also open, against index finger of first hand.

Shower

Rub both fists in a circular motion on your chest.

Cook/Kitchen

Lay both hands flat with fingers together. Flip the top hand from palm to back as if you're flipping a pancake. For kitchen, the flipping hand forms the letter "K" rather than remaining flat.

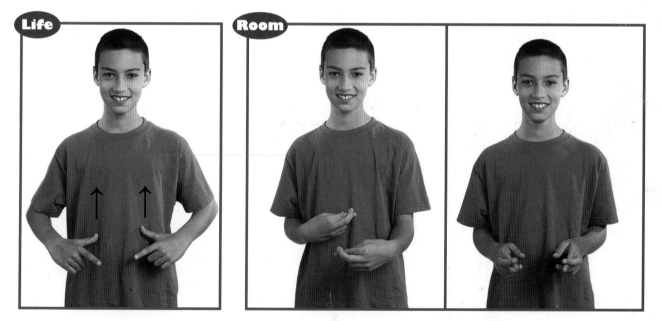

Life

Room

Living Room

1. LIFE: Move two "L" hand signs from your hips to your shoulders in front of your body.
2. ROOM: With two "R" hand signs, form the shape of a box, or room, to show two walls at a time.

Dining Room

1. **EAT:** With your thumb and fingertips of one hand together, touch your lips. 2. **ROOM:** With two "R" hand signs, form the shape of a box, or room, to show two walls at a time.

Bedroom

1. **BED:** Lean your head to one side and rest your ear against your palm as if you're going to sleep.
2. **ROOM:** With two "R" hand signs, form the shape of a box, or room, to show two walls at a time.

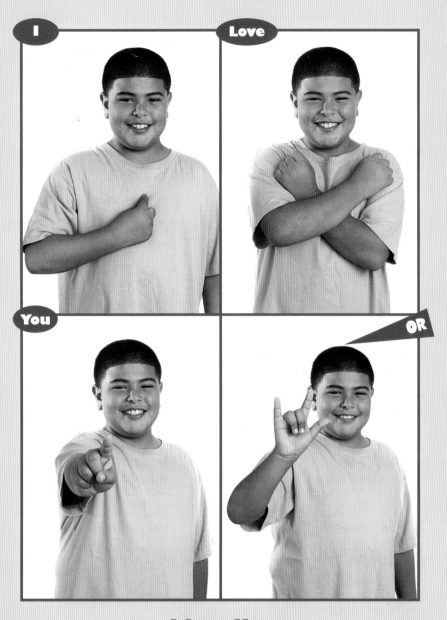

I Love You

1. Point to yourself. 2. Cross your arms with your fist touching the opposite shoulder, like a hug. 3. Point out to the person you love. OR: Use the "I Love You" hand sign: Have your thumb, index finger, and pinky finger up; your middle and ring fingers down. This comes from the letters I, L (for love), and Y (for you) all put together.

Dream

Form the letter "D" in one hand and touch the outside corner of your forehead. Move that hand outward, away from your head, with your index finger wiggling.

Dad

Open your hand and hold it sideways with your thumb touching your forehead.

Grandfather

Start with the sign for "Dad" and bounce it twice away from your body.

Great-Grandfather

Start with the sign for "Dad" and bounce it three times away from your body

Mom

Open your hand sideways with your thumb touching your chin.

Grandmother

Start with the sign for "Mom" and bounce it twice away from your body.

Great-Grandmother

Start with the sign for "Mom" and bounce it three times away from your body.

Baby

Move arms together as if you're holding and rocking a baby.

Boy

Grab the imaginary bill of a cap from your forehead and move out away from your head.

Girl

Use your thumb to trace your jaw line, or an old-fashioned bonnet string.

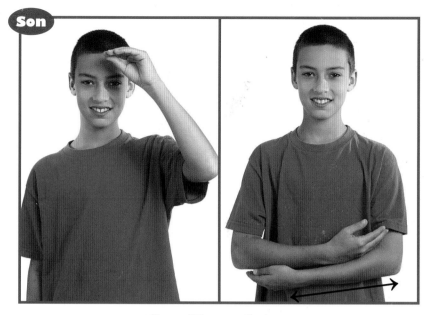

Son

Daughter

Son/Daughter

Begin with "Boy" or "Girl" sign and end with "Baby" sign.

Brother

Sister

Brother/Sister

Begin with a "Boy" or "Girl" sign. Then make a "I" sign with both hands and lay them sideways, one on top of the other.

Boy Cousin

Girl Cousin

Cousin

Form a "C" hand sign and move it in a circular motion near your forehead for a boy cousin or near your chin for a girl cousin.

Niece

Form an "N" hand sign and move it in a circular motion near your chin.

Aunt

Form an "A" hand sign and move it in a circular motion near your chin.

Uncle

Form a "U" hand sign and move it in a circular motion near your forehead.

Nephew

Form an "N" hand sign and move it in a circular motion near your forehead.

Cat

Trace imaginary whiskers on your face with one or two hands.

Dog

Tap your thigh and then snap your fingers with the same hand.

Like a frog's long tongue reaching out to catch a fly.

Frog

Pop your index and middle fingers out from under your chin.

Bird

Using your thumb and index finger, form a small beak at your mouth. Open and close.

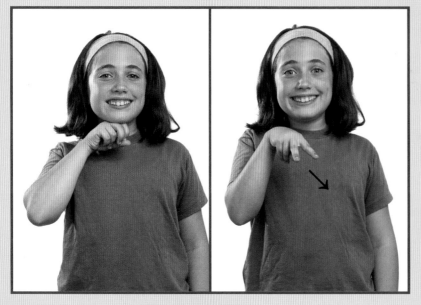

Lizard

Like the "Frog" sign, but pop your entire hand out from under your chin.

Just like a turtle's shell.

Like a fish.

Turtle

Hold one fist sideways and hide it under your other hand.

Fish

Hold your hand sideways and have it "swim" across you.

School

Just because you're supposed to be quiet doesn't mean you can't chat with your friends! One of the reasons sign language is great is that it allows you to talk in the library, at the movies, or even while eating. As a matter of fact, your school library is the perfect place to practice this next set of signs, since many relate to school and the classroom. But don't worry—you won't be graded on them!

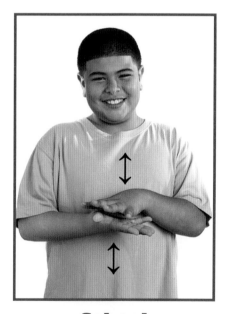

School

With one palm facing up and the other facing down, clap your hands twice.

Learn

Lay one hand flat with palm up. Your other hand takes something from your first hand and touches your head, as if you're putting information from a page into your brain.

Read

As if two eyes are reading the page.

Lay one hand flat with palm up. With the other hand, make a "V" hand sign and "scan" the opposite palm.

Teacher

Bring the fingertips of each hand to your temples and move your hands forward. Then have your palms face each other and move them downward to show a person.

Student

Form the sign for "Learn" (see page 23). Then have your palms face each other and move them downward to show a person.

Class

Begin with two "C" hand signs together, palms facing out. Move your hands away from each other, forming a circle in the air in front of you. End with your palms facing in.

Friends

Hook your index fingers together with one on top. Then switch to have the other on top.

Like a typewriter ribbon moving back and forth.

Pretend you're opening a book to read.

Computer

Form a "C" hand sign and slide it back and forth on the opposite forearm.

Books

Lay both hands together with palms flat and open.

Library

Form an "L" hand sign and make small circles in the air.

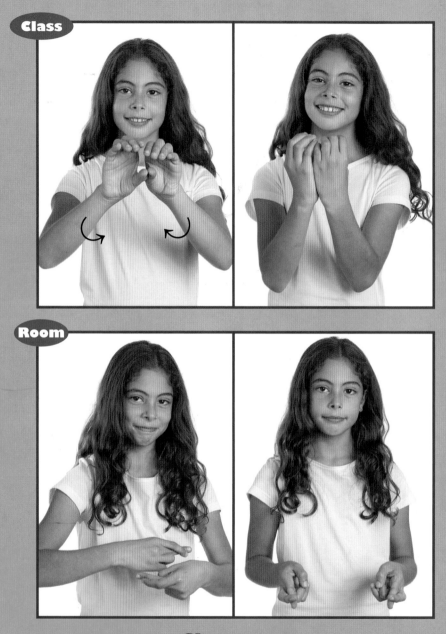

Class

Room

Classroom

1. **CLASS:** Begin with two "C" hand signs together, palms facing out. Move your hands away from each other, forming a circle in the air in front of you. End with your palms facing in. 2. **ROOM:** With two "R" hand signs, form the shape of a box, or room, to show two walls at a time.

Pen/Pencil

Pretend that you're writing.

Test

With the index finger of each hand, draw a question mark in the air in front of your shoulders or chest. Then open both hands and move them forward with your palms down.

Home **Work**

Homework

1. **HOME:** With your fingertips together, first touch the side of your mouth and then your temple.
2. **WORK:** Make fists with palms facing down. Place one wrist on top of the other.

Play

Time

Like you're pulling a string.

Diploma

Form two "F" hand signs. With your palms facing out, move your hands away from each other.

Recess

1. PLAY: Form two "Y" hand signs and wiggle them back and forth.
2. TIME: Then point your index finger to the opposite wrist.

Days of the Week

The **days of** the week are easy to learn because most begin with the first letter of the day followed by a small, circular sign. In no time, you can arrange a surprise birthday party for your best friend at school and she will never know.

As if the sun is setting.

Day

Form a "D" hand sign. Rest the elbow of your "D" hand on top of your other hand. Then bring your "D" hand down so that it rests on the opposite elbow.

Week

Move your index finger across the palm of your other hand.

Month

Form two "I" hand signs. Slide one index finger down the back of the other.

Year

Circle your two fists around each other once, then land one on top of the other.

Sunday

Open both hands with palms facing out. Make circles with both hands going in opposite directions.

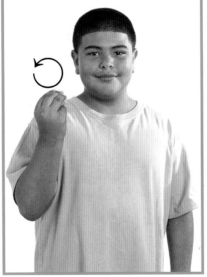

Monday

Form an "M" hand sign. With your palm facing up, move it in a small circle.

Tuesday

Form a "T" hand sign and move it in a small circle.

Wednesday

Form a "W" hand sign. With your palm facing up, move it in a small circle.

Thursday

Form an "H" hand sign. With your palm facing up, move it in a small circle.

Friday

Form an "F" hand sign and move it in a small circle.

Saturday

Form an "S" hand sign and move it in a small circle.

Colors

Once you've mastered the alphabet, learning colors is easy. Why? Because, like the signs for the days of the week in the last chapter, many of the colors shown here are represented in some way by their first letter. For example, with "red," you first make the letter "R." For "purple," you first make the letter "P," for green, the letter "G," and so on. Learning colors not only helps your signing to become more descriptive, but it's also great for when you want to coordinate your outfits with a friend!

Colors

Form a "5" hand sign with your palm facing in. Wiggle your fingers at your chin.

Red

Form the letter "R," then touch your lips twice with your index finger.

As if you're squeezing an orange

Orange

Open and close your fist near your mouth and nose.

Yellow

Form the letter "Y" and twist it near your shoulder.

Green

Form the letter "G" and twist it in front of your body.

Blue

Form the letter "B" and twist it near your shoulder.

Purple

Form the letter "P" and have it dance in the air.

Pink

Form the letter "P," then touch your lips twice with the middle finger.

Brown

Form the letter "B" and move it up and down along your cheek near the corner of your mouth.

As if you're picking something off your shirt.

Black

Draw your index finger along your forehead or eyebrows.

White

Lay your hand on your chest and then move it outward into a flat "O" shape.

Gold

Silver

Gold/Silver

Touch your earlobe with your middle finger and then wiggle that hand down into the letter "Y" for gold, or "S" for silver.

Feelings

ost of these signs sort of look like the feelings they represent. The expressiveness in ASL allows the language to really speak for itself. The meaning of a sentence can change by simply changing the expression on your face. Remember to show the matching emotion on your face as you use these signs.

Feelings

With an open palm, touch your chest with your middle finger. Then bring your hand slightly up and away from your body.

Happy

With open hands, rub your chest in an upward motion.

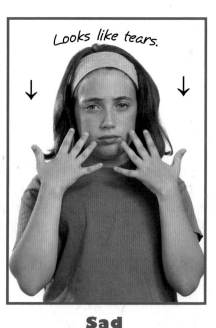

Looks like tears.

Sad

Open both hands in front of your face and move them slightly downward from your eyebrows to your cheekbones.

Angry

Form a "5" hand sign in front of your face and bend your fingers as if you're pulling something sticky away.

Bored

Touch your index finger outside of your nostril and then twist it slightly outward.

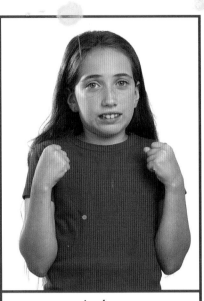

As if you just got scared!

Scared

Make two fists near your chest and then open your hands.

Curious

Form an "F" hand sign and touch your neck with your thumb and forefinger.

Excited

With your palms open, alternate touching your chest with each middle finger.

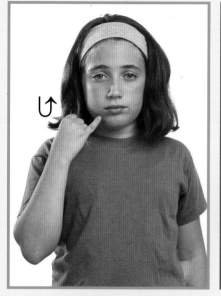

Jealous

Form the letter "J" at the corner of your mouth.

Frustrated

Form a "B" hand sign and press the back of that hand into your chin a few times.

Proud

Form an "A" hand sign and then move your thumb from your belly button up to your chest.

Playful/Silly

Form a "Y" hand sign. Touch your nose with your thumb and then wiggle your hand down and away from your face in a wavy, diagonal line.

Showing you have a dry throat.

Thirsty

Move your index finger down your neck from under your chin to your throat.

Tired

Touch the back of your fingertips to your chest near your underarms. Then fold your body over so that the back of your hands meet in front of your chest.

Hungry

Form a "C" hand sign. With your fingertips touching your chest, move from your neckline down to above your belly button.

Favorite Foods

As you learn a few signs, you will quickly realize that sign language really makes a lot of sense. The sign you make somehow reminds you of the word you're trying to say. Many of the food signs in this chapter look like their word. If you want popcorn during a movie, just move your index fingers up and down as if they're popcorn popping. If you want milk, pretend you're milking a cow. Do you have a favorite food? You can start there and create a café or market in your own home—all in sign language. Someday, if you ever work in a restaurant or grocery store, you'll have a head start when someone who is deaf comes in to eat or shop.

As if you're about to put food into your mouth.

Food
With all your fingertips touching, move your hand to your lips.

French **Toast**

French Fries

Form an "F" hand sign with your palm facing down in front of your body. Bounce it twice to one side of your body.

French Toast

1. FRENCH: Form an "F" hand sign and dip it down and back up as if you're sewing. 2. TOAST: Form a "V" hand sign. Use the fingertips to touch the palm and back of the opposite hand, as if you're sticking a fork into a slice of bread.

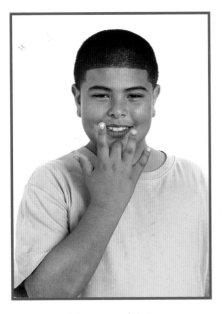

Imagine you are making the links of a sausage.

Favorite

Form a "5" hand sign, then touch your chin with your middle finger.

Hot Dog

Beginning with both hands in front of your body, move them away from each other as you open and close your hands.

Pizza

Form a "P" hand sign and draw a Z in the air in front of your body.

As if they are kernels popping.

Popcorn

Make two fists with palms facing in. Alternate lifting up your index fingers.

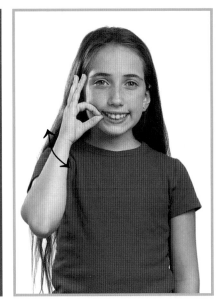

Fruit

Form an "F" hand sign. Touch your index finger and thumb to the corner of your mouth and wiggle.

Cereal

Pretend that you're eating cereal: one hand is the bowl and use two fingers for the spoon.

Meat **Balls**

As if you're holding a ball between them.

Meatballs

1. **MEAT:** With your thumb and index finger, hold the area between the thumb and index finger of your other hand. Move your hands slightly.
2. **BALL:** Move both hands to and fro together.

Spaghetti

Move both pinky fingers in a circular motion on either side of your face as if you're twirling a long piece of pasta.

Hamburger

Cup your hands together as if you're holding a burger between them. Then turn your hands over so that the bottom hand is now on top.

Cheese

Hamburger

Cheeseburger

1. CHEESE: Twist the heel of one palm against the other a few times. 2. BURGER: Form the sign for "Hamburger."

As if you're licking something sweet.

Ice Cream

Pretend that you're holding and licking an ice cream cone.

Candy

Form a "U" hand sign. Brush the fingertips over your lips a few times.

As if you're milking a cow.

Water

Form a "W" hand sign and touch your chin with your index finger.

Milk

Open and close your fists.

Juice

Use your pinky finger to draw the letter "J" at the corner of your mouth.

Soda

Dip your middle finger in and out of the fist of your other hand. Then place your top hand flat on top of your fist.

Sports and Hobbies

Sports, such as baseball, have their own sign language among the players and coaches. These signs can be complicated. In fact, teams can have an entire book of these secret signals. When you're practicing with your team, you can use signs to communicate to your teammates.

Signing also comes in handy if you're putting on a play and you need to communicate quietly backstage. You may also have an interpreter—someone near the stage signing what the actor is saying to the audience in case someone watching is deaf.

Like a hockey stick.

Hockey
Form an "X" hand sign. With the knuckle down, sweep that hand over the opposite palm.

Tennis

Pretend that you're holding a tennis racket and hitting a forehand.

Swimming

Pretend that you're swimming the breast stroke.

Baseball

Pretend that you're about to swing a baseball bat.

As if you're kicking a ball.

To show the strings on a football.

Basketball

Pretend you're holding a basketball and you're getting ready to make a basket.

Soccer

Bend your arms. Use one hand to hit the palm of your other hand.

Football

Interlace your fingers together two times.

Pretend they're blades moving along the ice.

As if you're skiing.

Skating

Form two "X" hand signs with your palms up. Alternate moving your hands away from your body.

Skateboarding

Form two "B" hand signs with palms down. Repeat sliding one hand forward and the other hand back.

Skiing

Form two "S" hand signs with palms facing in. Move your hands down and back.

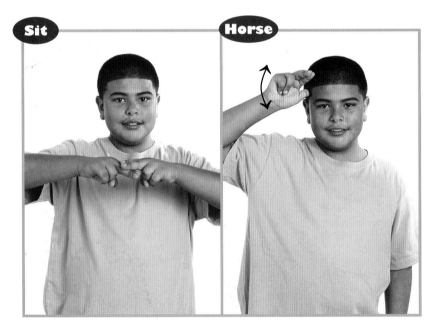

Sit

Horse

Riding

1. SIT: Form two "U" hand signs. Place the index and middle fingers of one hand on top of the other. 2. HORSE: Form an "H" hand sign. Have it facing out and pointing up on one side of your forehead (like a horse's ear). Then move your fingers down and up twice.

Game/Challenge

Form two "A" hand signs and tap the knuckles together.

Team

Form two "T" hand signs. Bring them together at the thumbs, then circle them in front of you until your pinkies meet.

Art/Drawing

Form an "I" hand sign. Draw a zigzag line with your pinky finger across the palm of your other hand.

Your hand is like the canvas.

Painting

Brush the fingertips of one hand across the palm of the opposite hand. Make sure the opposite palm is standing sideways.

As if you're holding a camera.

Photography

Hold one "C" hand sign next to your cheek with fingers pointing out. Then move your hand and place the thumb side against the opposite outward facing flat palm.

Sewing

Pretend that you're stitching something with a needle and thread.

Poetry

Bring one arm out and with palm up. Form a "P" hand sign with the other hand and sweep a figure 8 pattern.

Stage

Have both palms facing down. Form an "S" hand sign and sweep it over the other arm from elbow to fingertips. Imagine an actor moving across the surface of a stage.

Drama/Theater

Alternate moving two "A" hand signs in a circular motion toward your chest or shoulders.

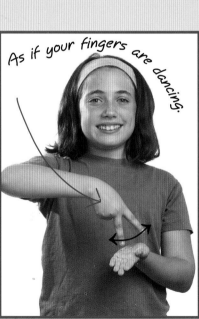

As if your fingers are dancing.

Dance

Move an upside down "V" hand sign from side to side over the palm of your opposite hand.

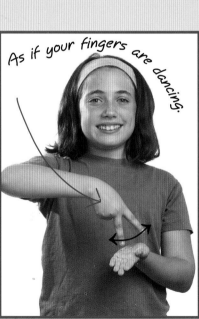

48 **Sign Language for Kids**

Musical Instruments

You can play every instrument in your own band when you sign them—and they can sound exactly the way you want them to! These signs will be useful to teach other students in your music class or ensemble.

To show that the sound of your voice is traveling away from you.

Music

Bring one arm forward with your palm up. Sweep the other open hand above that arm in a figure 8 pattern.

Voice

Touch the fingertips of a "V" hand sign to your throat and then move your hand out.

Guitar

Pretend that you're playing a guitar.

Piano

Pretend that you're playing a keyboard in front of you.

As if you're playing the slide.

Trombone

Pretend that you're holding a trombone. Move one hand back and forth.

Flute

Pretend that you're playing a flute. Have one palm facing in, the other facing out.

Trumpet

Pretend that you're holding a trumpet. Move your fingers up and down as if you're playing different notes.

Cello

Pretend that you're holding a cello between your legs. Use either hand to hold the bow.

Drums

Act as if you're beating a drum with your hands flat or by pretending that you're holding drumsticks.

Violin

Pretend that you're playing a violin. Tuck the violin under your chin and hold it with your left hand. Pretend you have the bow in your right hand.

Transportation and Travel

Every spoken language has its own sign language, but the signs of each tend to have more similarities than the words. For example, if you travel to France and meet someone who is deaf, you would understand him or her quicker by signing than by one of you speaking French and the other English. French Sign Language and ASL are the most similar. Spanish sign language and ASL also have more similarities than spoken English and Spanish. Surprisingly, British Sign Language and ASL are quite different even though English is spoken in both countries. Either way, here are some basic signs for traveling around your own area or somewhere new.

As if you're wearing suspenders.

Vacation
With open hands, hook your thumbs near your shoulders.

Travel

Form a "V" hand sign and move it forward in a wavy motion.

Visit

Form two "V" hand signs and have your palms facing you. Alternate moving each hand in a circular motion toward your body.

Airplane

Form the sign for "I Love You" (see page 17) and pretend that hand is flying through the air.

Train

Form two "U" hand signs. Slide the first two fingers of one hand back and forth over the first two fingers of the other hand.

Bus

Form two "B" hand signs and have your palms facing you. Place one hand on top of the other.

Car

Pretend that you're driving a car.

As if you're pedaling a bicycle.

Like it's the propeller moving.

Bicycle

Make two fists and take turns moving them around in circles.

Boat

Cup your hands to make a boat. Then move your hands forward with a wavy motion.

Helicopter

Place the palm of one hand on top of the index finger of your other hand. Wiggle the top hand slightly.

Mountains

Form two "S" hand signs and sit one on top of the other. With palms still facing down, open your hands and move them up and out in a wavy motion. This sign shows the rocks along a mountain.

Beach

Bend one arm near your chest. With the other hand, rub your elbow up toward your hand as if you're wiping off sand.

Camping

With your fists facing each other, stretch out your index and pinky fingers. Touch these two fingers of one hand to the same two fingers of the other hand, then move both hands down and apart a few times to make the shape of a tent.

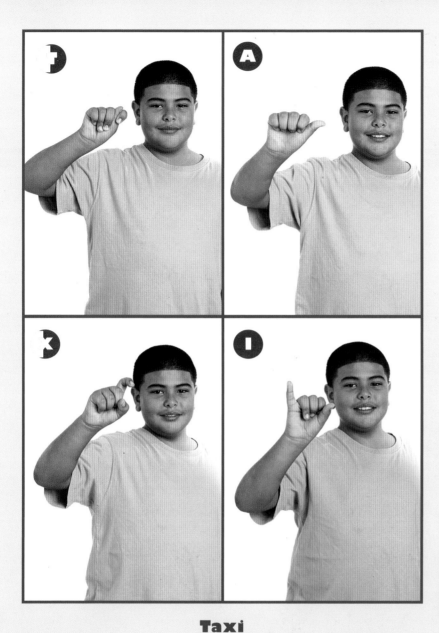

Taxi

Fingerspell T-A-X-I.

Truck

Pretend that you're driving a truck. The steering wheel should be larger than the steering wheel of a car.

Animals

nimals, **such as** apes, sea lions, and dogs, can be taught sign language. In fact, the next time you visit your local zoo, try to catch the sea lions at feeding time. You will see the zookeepers using basic signs to communicate with them. If you visit an aquarium and see a show there, you will also find the trainers using signs with the dolphins and killer whales. With your knowledge of sign language, you might be able to understand some of the things they are saying.

Animals
Touch the front of your shoulders with the fingertips of each hand and bring your hands toward and away from each other.

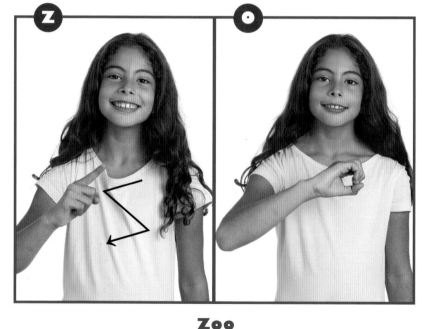

Zoo
Fingerspell Z-O-O.

Gorilla

Beat your chest several times with your fists.

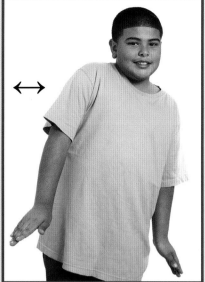

Penguin

With arms alongside your body and your palms facing the ground, move from side to side like a penguin.

To show the stripes of a zebra.

Zebra

Start with both hands open and palms toward your chest. Bend and straighten your fingers several times.

Monkey

Alternate moving your fingertips from your hips up to your under-arms.

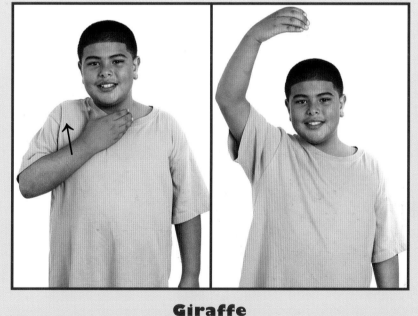

Giraffe

Form a "C" hand sign with your palm facing you. Move your hand from the base of your neck up past your head, like the long neck of a giraffe.

Elephant

Form a "C" hand sign with your palm facing you. Bring your hand from the tip of your nose downward in the shape of an elephant's trunk.

Like the large whiskers of a tiger.

Tiger

Start with both hands open and palms toward your cheeks. Bend and straighten your fingers several times.

As if you are brushing the lion's mane.

Lion

Place your hand over your head and move it from the top of your forehead to the back of your neck.

Farm

Open your hand, then move from one side of your chin to the other with your thumb nearest you.

Cow

Form a "Y" hand sign and have the thumb touching the top side of your head. Move your palm slightly back and forth to show the cow's horn.

As if showing the horns.

Goat

Make a fist under your chin and pull downward as if stroking a beard. Then make a "V" hand sign and place the back of that hand against your forehead.

Horse

Form an "H" hand sign. Have it facing out and pointing up on one side of your forehead (like a horse's ear). Then move your fingers down and up twice.

Sheep

Form a "2" hand sign with your palm facing up. Move your hand up the opposite forearm, from your wrist to your elbow, as if you're shearing the wool of a sheep.

Duck

Make a duck's bill by opening and closing your hand in front of your mouth.

Rooster

Form a "3" hand sign, then touch the center of your forehead with your thumb. Slightly bend your index and middle fingers twice.

Pig

Place the back of your hand under your chin, with palm facing down, and wiggle your fingers.

Mouse

Gently but quickly touch the side your nose with your index finger a few times.

Clothing

Trying to decide what to wear today? Want to tell your friend across the room what you plan to wear to the party this afternoon? Can you describe what your teacher is wearing, or let your friend know you're referring to the girl in the yellow shirt and blue pants?

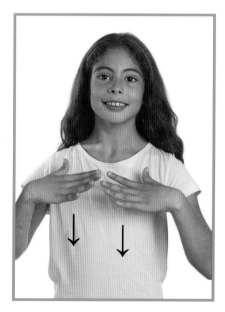

Get Dressed

With your hands open, brush your thumbs against the front of your shoulders at the same time in a downward motion.

Change

Form two "X" hand signs and place one palm over the other palm. Twist your wrists while turning your hands. The top hand then becomes the bottom hand.

Hat

Tap the top of your head or pretend that you're putting on a hat.

Jacket

Pretend that you're putting on a jacket.

Shoes

Make two fists with palms facing down. Tap your fists together twice at the center of your body.

Shirt

Form two "F" hand signs. Use your thumb and index finger to grab a part of your shirt (near your shoulders).

Pants/Dress

For "Pants," rub both hands downward from your thighs toward your knees. "Dress" is the same movement except you start from your shoulders and go down toward your knees.

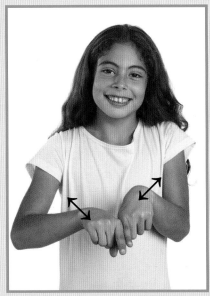

Socks

Stretch out your index fingers and rub them up and down against each other near your feet.

Senses

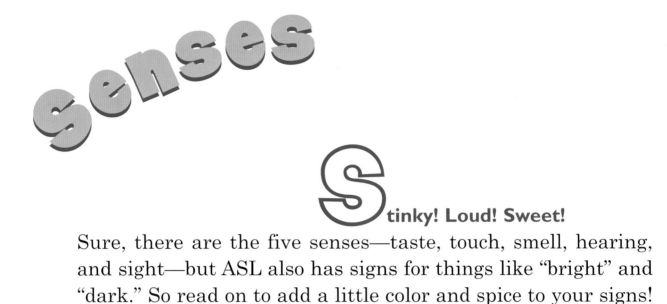

Stinky! Loud! Sweet!

Sure, there are the five senses—taste, touch, smell, hearing, and sight—but ASL also has signs for things like "bright" and "dark." So read on to add a little color and spice to your signs!

Sight (See)
Form a "V" hand sign. Touch the top of your cheekbone with your middle finger and then move your hand outward.

Sound (Hear)
Point your index finger toward your earlobe.

Smell
Sniff your palm as it moves to and from your nose.

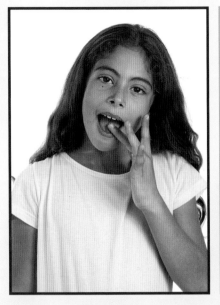

Taste

Pretend to touch your tongue with your index finger.

Touch

Use your middle finger to touch the back of your other hand.

Stinky

Sniff your palm as it moves to and from your nose. Make a face to show that something smells bad.

Dark

Cross the fingers of your right and left hands in front of your face as if you're drawing a curtain in front of your eyes.

Bright (Clear)

Bring the fingertips of both hands together. Then open both hands out to the sides with your palms facing forward.

64 Sign Language for Kids

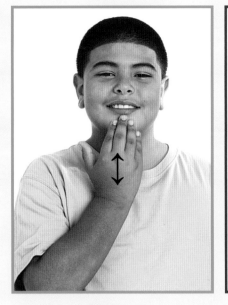

Sweet

Brush your fingertips down over your lips a few times as if you're licking something sweet off your fingertips.

Sour
(Bitter, Tart)

Touch your index finger to your chin and twist it several times. Make a face to show that something tasted sour.

As if you're sprinkling salt into your food.

Salt(y)

Form a "V" in one hand and an "H" in the other. Tap the fingertips of your "V" hand over the fingers of your "H" hand.

Smooth

With both palms facing down, slide one palm over the back of the opposite hand to show its smooth surface.

Rough

Slide the fingertips of one hand in a wavy motion along the palm of the opposite hand.

Loud

Touch each earlobe with your index finger. Then open and move both hands up and down near your shoulders.

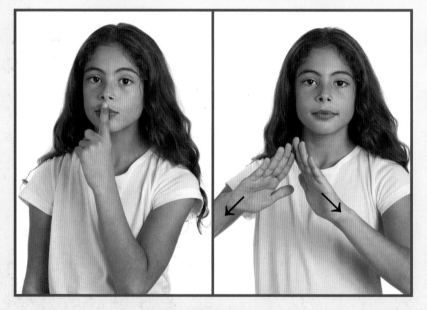

Quiet

Bring your index finger to your lips, as if you're asking someone to be quiet. Then place your hands at an angle to each other with palms facing out. Move both hands down and out to the side.

Holidays and Religions

Some congregations have quite a number of deaf members. Because of this, there are sign language interpreters during many services. Other houses of worship even have a deaf minister or leader because they have a full deaf congregation. If you sing in the choir at your congregation, you may learn enough signs from this book to include in a song.

Religion

Form an "R" hand sign and bring it to your chest over your heart. Then turn your hand out away from your chest.

As if you're stroking a small beard.

Jewish

Bring the fingertips of one hand together and then touch your chin.

Muslim

Form two "M" hand signs and hold them at the sides of your forehead with palms facing down. Then move both hands down at the same time to the sides of your chin.

Baptist

Form two "A" hand signs and hold them forward with palms facing each other. Then twist your wrists in both directions.

To show the Buddha's belly.

Buddhist

Place your hand flat above your stomach and move it in a circular motion.

Catholic

Form a "U" hand sign and use your fingertips to trace the shape of a cross on your forehead.

Jesus

Hold your hands open with the palms facing each other. Touch the tip of your middle finger to the palm of the opposite hand. Repeat, using the other middle finger.

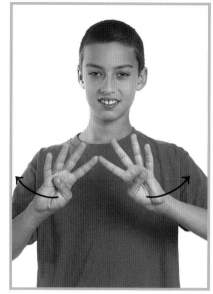

Bible

1. JESUS: Hold your hands open with palms facing each other. Touch the tip of your middle finger to the palm of the opposite hand. Repeat using the other middle finger. 2. BOOK: Lay both hands together with palms flat and open, as if you're opening a book to read.

Chanukah

Form two "4" hands and hold them in front of your chest with your palms facing out. Move both hands at the same time to the sides in small arcs to show the shape of the menorah.

Passover

Form an "S" in each hand. Hold one hand near your chest with your palm facing out. Use the thumb of your other hand to tap your elbow. This is a lot like the sign for "Cracker." It suggests the matzoh eaten during this holiday.

God

Open your hand and have the palm facing sideways. Reach your hand up toward the sky and then bring it down to about shoulder level.

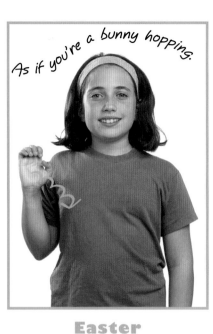

As if you're a bunny hopping.

Easter

Form an "E" hand sign and hold in front of your shoulder. Then bounce your hand forward away from your body.

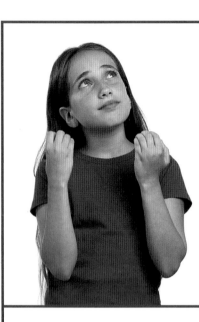

Heaven

Hold both hands to chin level with fingers bent. Move your hands upward and toward your body in a circular motion, then turn your palms out and upward toward the sky.

Prayer

Bring your hands together with your palms touching. Move your hands toward your body while you slightly bow your head down.

Christmas

Begin with a "C" hand sign in front of your opposite shoulder. Then move it in an arc shape until it is in front of your other shoulder.

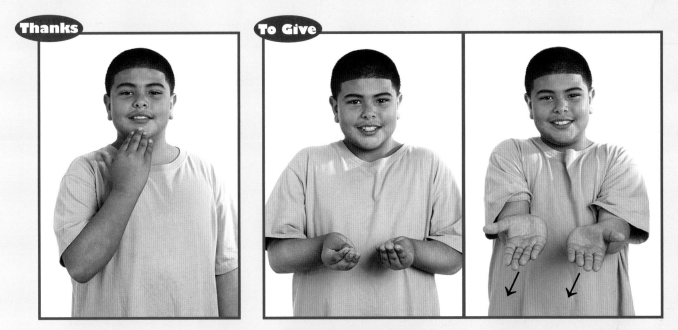

Thanks

To Give

Thanksgiving

1. **THANKS:** Touch your chin with your fingertips and then move both hands away from your body.
2. **TO GIVE:** With your palms still facing up, bring your fingers together, as if you're holding something. Then move your hands forward while opening them, as if you're giving something away.

To show the white collar worn by a minister.

Celebrate

Form two "X" hand signs and have your palms facing you. Move your hands in small circular motions on either side of your forehead.

Minister/Priest

Form a "G" hand sign. Trace your fingertips from the middle of your neck outward.

Church
Form a "C" hand sign and, using the thumb, tap the top of your other hand a few times.

Synagogue
Form an "S" hand sign and tap the top of your other hand a few times.

This shows the rabbi's prayer shawl or tallis.

Rabbi
Form two "R" hand signs. Touch the fingertips of both hands to each side of your chest and then move them down to your stomach.

Doctor's Office and Health

It's no fun when you feel sick. You might feel so bad that you are too tired to tell your brothers and sisters what hurts or what happened at the doctor's office. This next set of signs will help you tell them without having to speak. Maybe you want to be a doctor or dentist some day. It is always a good idea to learn some signs in case you have deaf patients.

Pain
Move your index fingers toward each other as you twist your hands from side to side. Use this sign near any part of your body that hurts or has an injury.

Dentist
Form a "D" hand sign. Tap your teeth with all of your fingertips except your index finger.

Sick
Touch your forehead with the middle fingertip of one hand and your stomach with the middle fingertip of the other hand.

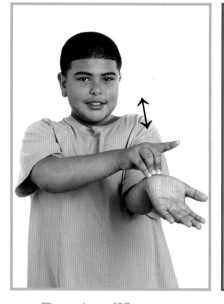

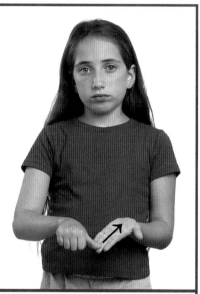

Doctor/Nurse

Form a "D" hand sign and use all of your fingertips, except your index finger, to tap the wrist of your other hand. The motion shows you checking your pulse. "Nurse" is the same movement as "Doctor," but use an "N" hand sign instead of "D."

Hospital/Patient

Form an "H" hand sign and use your fingertips to trace the shape of a cross on your opposite upper arm. "Patient" is the same movement as "Hospital," but use a "P" hand sign instead of an "H."

As if you're giving yourself a shot.

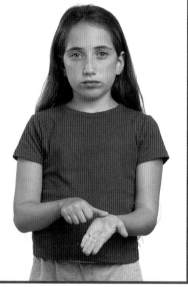

Shot

Form an "L" hand sign. Use the index finger to touch the top of the arm.

Medicine

Move the tip of your middle finger in small circles on the palm of your opposite hand.

Operation

Use your thumb to draw a line up the palm of your other hand. Begin at your fingertips and end at your wrist. This sign can also be done anywhere on your body that will have an operation.

Body

Lay both hands flat on your upper chest and then move them downward to touch your lower chest area (close to your waistline).

Bones

Use your index finger to tap the back fist of your other hand.

Brain

Tap the middle of your forehead with your index finger several times.

Heart

Touch your heart with the tip of your middle finger.

This sign shows you breathing in and out.

Breath/Breathe

Lay both hands flat on your chest, one hand above the other. Move your hands together to and from your body a few times.

Cold/Flu

Using the index finger and thumb of one hand, move up and down under your nose as if you're wiping a runny nose.

This shows blood dripping from a wound.

Blood

Touch your lips with your index finger to show the color red. Then hold both open hands in front of your chest with palms facing in. Wiggle the fingertips of one hand as you brush them down across the back of your other hand.

As if you're holding in a sneeze.

Cough

Lay your hand over your chest and tap it several times.

Sneeze

Place your index finger under your nose.

Dizzy

With your fingers bent and palm facing you, move your hand in a circular motion in front of your face.

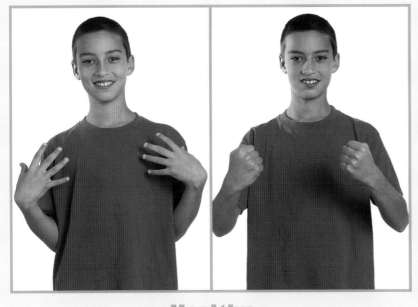

Healthy

With your fingers slightly bent and palms facing you, touch your shoulders/chest area. Then bring your hands forward as you close them into fists.

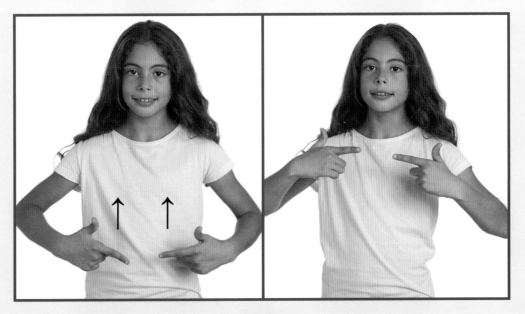

Life

Form two "L" hand signs with palms facing in. Move them from your waistline to your shoulders at the same time.

Nature, Weather, and Seasons

You can sign the latest weather report or things you see on a camping trip. There are also many beautiful songs to sign using this vocabulary from nature and the outdoor world around you.

Nature
Form an "N" in one hand and an "S" in the other. Move the "N" hand in a small circle above the "S" hand before landing on it.

Like a tree moving in the wind.

Trees
Open your hand near your head. Rest your elbow on the back of your other hand. Twist your wrist and wiggle the fingers near your head.

Earth
Form an "S" hand sign with your palm facing down. Sit the tips of your thumb and middle finger of your other hand on the back of your "S" hand and rock it back and forth to show a globe spinning.

This sign shows smelling a flower, or "rosy" cheeks.

Flowers

Bring all your fingertips together and use them to touch each cheek once.

Stars

Rub your index fingers up and down against each other as you raise your hands.

Moon

Hold a "C" hand sign up near the top of your head.

Sun

Use your index finger to trace a circle in the air near you head and then open your hand.

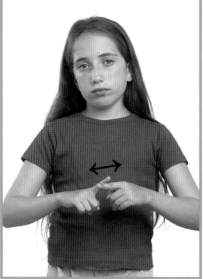

Weather

Form two "W" hand signs and have them face each other. Bring them together to touch at the thumb/pinky, then twist your wrists from side to side.

Temperature

Begin with two "I" hand signs. Slide one index finger up and down the other index finger.

Clouds/Storm

With your palms facing each other and fingers bent, move your hands in a circular motion to show clouds in the sky. Use stronger movements for a storm.

Like you are shivering from the cold.

Hot

Hold your thumb and fingertips toward your mouth, then twist your hand away quickly with your palm facing down. The sign looks as though you're about to bite into something but it's too hot, so you pull it away.

Cold/Winter

Form two "S" hand signs with palms facing each other. Hold them near your chest and shake them.

Rain

1. **WATER:** Form the letter "W" and touch your chin with your index finger. 2. With palms down and fingers bent, move your hands downward while your fingers open and close.

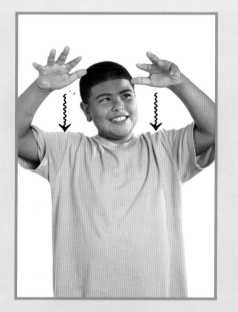

Snow

With palms facing the ground, move your hands down while your fingers gently wiggle.

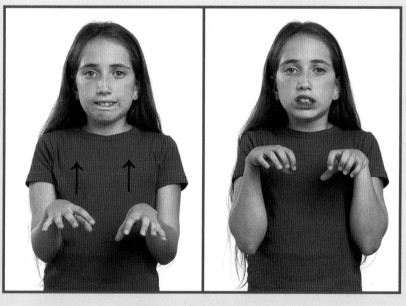

Ice/Freeze

Open both hands with palms down and fingers slightly bent. Then pull them toward you as you curl your fingers even more.

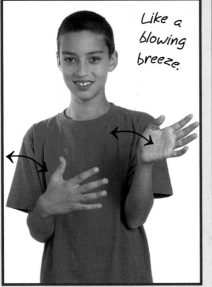

Like a blowing breeze.

Wind

Hold both hands in front of you with your palms facing each other. Move your hands from side to side.

Lightning

Point your index finger to the sky and move it downward with a quick, zigzag motion.

Colors

Imagine forming a rainbow in the sky.

Rainbow

1. COLORS: Form a "5" hand sign with your palm facing in. Wiggle your fingers at your chin. 2. Lay your palm open and move it in an upward arc shape from the opposite side of your body to the same side while wiggling the fingers of your other hand above it.

Season

Open one hand flat with palm facing forward. With the other hand, form an "S" hand sign and move the thumb side in a circle on the open palm.

As if a flower is blooming.

Spring/Grass

Form a "C" hand sign with your thumb near your body. With the thumb and fingertips of your other hand together, move your hand upward through the "C" hand. Then open your fingers. "Grass" is the same movement except don't open your fingers.

The movement suggests leaves falling from the trees.

Pretend you're wiping the sweat off your brow.

Fall/Autumn

Draw your arm across your chest with your hand open and flat near your shoulder. With the other open hand, wiggle your fingers while moving your hand along the opposite forearm near your elbow.

Summer

Draw your index finger across your forehead.

Nature, Weather, and Seasons 83

Practical Words and Question Words

This next set of signs will help you to make your conversations feel more complete. You know it's important to be polite. There are also times when you might need help or when you need to ask for something.

Please/Sorry

With one hand, rub your chest in a circular motion toward your shoulder. "Sorry" is the same movement but with an "S" hand sign.

Thank you

Touch your chin with the fingertips of one hand and then move that hand away from your body.

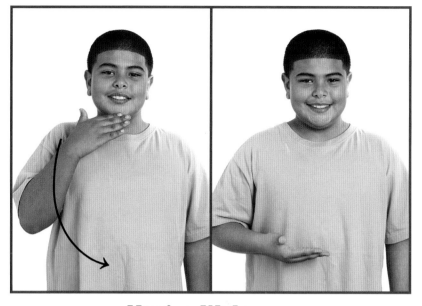

You're Welcome

Form the sign for "Thank you," but keep your hand moving in an arc toward your waist.

Help

Form a "10" hand sign and place it sideways on your other open palm. Then move both hands upward. Move your hands toward yourself to ask for help. Move your hands toward a friend to offer help.

More

Bring all the fingertips of both hands together in front of your body.

Finished

Form two "5" hand signs with your palms facing in. Bring your hands to the sides of your face and then shake them away from you so that your palms face out.

Want

Begin with your hands out, palms facing up and fingers bent. Move both hands toward your body, as if you're pulling something toward you or opening a drawer.

Patience

Form an "A" hand sign and rub your chin with your thumb in a downward motion.

As if you're keeping a secret.

Private

Form an "A" hand sign and tap your thumb against your closed lips.

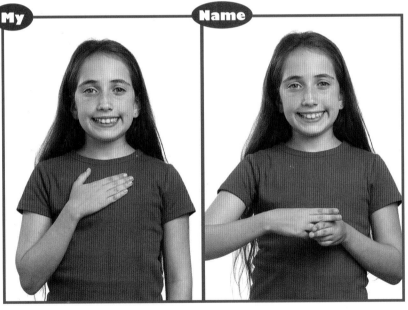

My   Name

My Name (is)

1. **MY:** Touch your chest with an open palm. 2. **NAME:** Form two "H" hand signs. Rest the extended fingers of one hand on the fingers of the other hand.

As if a head is nodding.

Yes

Form an "S" hand sign and bend at the wrist.

No

Open and close your index and middle finger over your thumb at least twice.

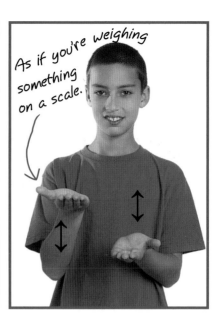

As if you're weighing something on a scale.

Maybe

Have both hands flat and open with your palms facing up. Alternate moving them up and down.

Me Too

Form a "Y" hand sign and move it to and fro between yourself and another (even an imaginary) person.

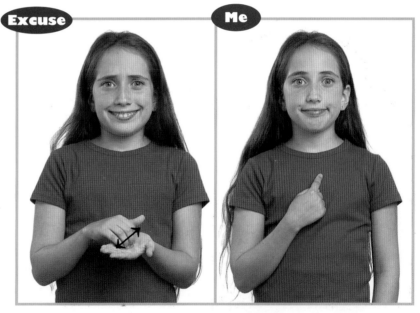

Excuse **Me**

Excuse Me

1. EXCUSE: Rub the fingertips of one hand back and forth against the open palm of your other hand. 2. ME: Point to yourself.

Practical Words and Question Words 87

Like a lightbulb being turned on.

Understand

Place your fist near the side of your forehead. Pop your index finger up and down. If you shake your head, it means you don't understand.

Who

Form an "L" hand sign with your palm facing sideways. Touch your chin with your thumb. Then bend and straighten your index finger a few times.

What

Open both hands flat with palms facing up. Alternate moving them forward and back in front of your body.

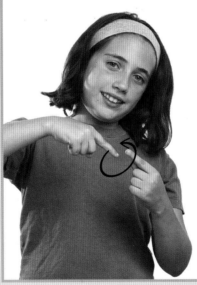

When

Form two "I" hand signs. Circle one index finger around the other to show the hands on a clock going around.

Where

With your palm facing out, shake your index finger from side to side near your shoulder.

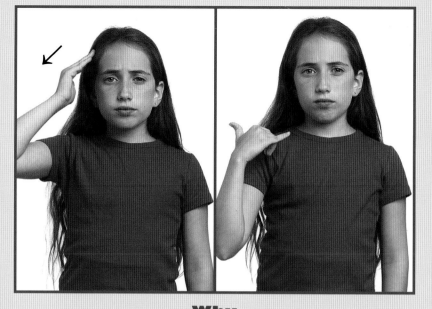

Why

Touch your head with the fingertips of your hand, then move that hand down and away into a "Y" hand sign.

How

Hold both hands curved with your knuckles touching and fingertips pointing into your chest. Then turn one or both palms up while keeping your fingers curved.

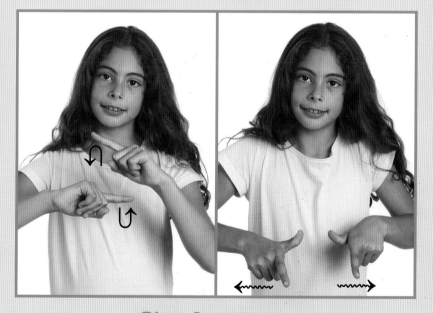

Sign Language

1. SIGN: Circle your index fingers toward your body. 2. LANGUAGE: Form two "L" hands with palms facing down in front of you. Wiggle your hands and move them away from each other.

Linking Words

Every now and then you may find yourself in need of these few signs that help you to form a sentence.

As if you're weighing something on a scale.

If

Form two "F" hand signs with your palms facing in. Alternate moving your hands up and down.

And

Bring your open hand sideway across your body. Then move your hand back to its own side while closing all your fingers together.

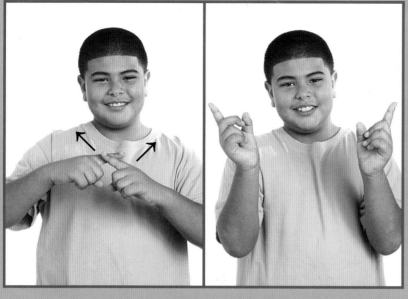

But

Cross your index fingers near your fingertips and then separate them.

Or/Which

Form two "A" hand signs with thumbs pointing up. Alternate moving your hands up and down in front of your body.

With

Form two "A" hands with thumbs pointing up. Bring your hands together in front of you.

Making Sentences

Just as every spoken language has its own word order, so does sign language. For example, in Spanish, you describe a "blue ball" as a "ball blue." In American Sign Language, sentences are formed in the following order:

T: Time
N: Noun
A: Adjective
V: Verb

This is different than how we form regular English sentences. For example:

	Verb		Adj.	Noun	Time
English:	*Throw*	*the*	*blue*	*ball*	*now.*

	Time	Noun	Adj.	Verb
ASL:	*Now*	*ball*	*blue*	*throw.*

	Verb		Adj.	Noun	Time
English:	*Read*	*the*	*short*	*story*	*first.*

	Time	Noun	Adj.	Verb
ASL:	*First*	*story*	*short*	*read.*

Because English sentences and ASL sentences are formed differently, some schools for deaf students teach reading and writing classes in English word order instead of ASL order. This has helped deaf students from other countries develop better reading and writing skills in English.

Can you form the following sentences in ASL using the words you learned in this book?

1. Is Dad tired?

2. Is there more pizza?

3. Where is your guitar?

4. Where are my socks and shoes?

5. I have a cold.

6. My name is _____.

7. I understand.

8. School will finish on Friday.

9. The juice is sour.

10. Thanksgiving is on Saturday.

Answers:

1. Dad tired? (Raise your eyebrows.)
2. Pizza more? (Raise your eyebrows.)
3. Guitar yours where? (Raise your eyebrows.)
4. Socks shoes mine where? (Raise your eyebrows.)
5. Me cold.
6. Me name (fingerspell your name).
7. Me understand. (Nod your head.)
8. Friday school finish.
9. Juice sour.
10. Saturday Thanksgiving.

Index

Lora F. Heller, MS, MT-BC, is a board certified music therapist, master's level teacher of the deaf, creator of New York City's Baby Fingers sign language and arts program (www.mybabyfingers.com), and mommy to Ezekiel and Ossian. She has worked with children of all ages and abilities, providing language stimulation and developmental growth through music, theater, and sign language. Her research and writing has been published in parenting magazines as well as college textbooks. Lora has produced sign language and music instructional videos and DVDs with her husband, Ian Lowell Heller, producer and composer of children's music and related media. Their children's music CDs, without signs, are also available. Their band is called Stinky Feet.